Argentinean Asado

Tips and Secrets for the Best Asado

emecé editores

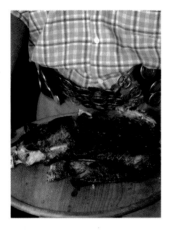

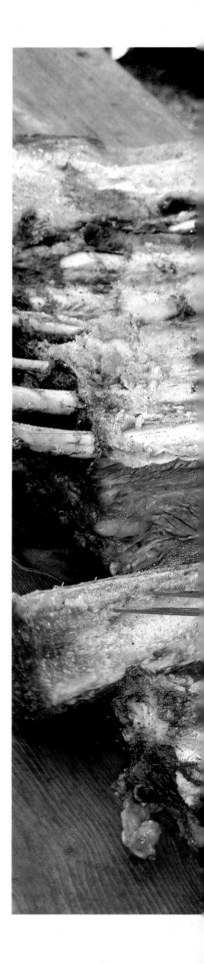

Argentinean Asado / edición a cargo de
Ricardo Sabanes.- 1ª ed. – Buenos Aires :
Emecé, 2004.
    72 p. ; 30x17 cm.

    ISBN 950-04-2587-4

    1. Cocina al Asador I. Sabanes,
Ricardo, ed.
        CDD 641.76

Diseño: Valeria Macchia

**Banco de Contenidos del
Grupo Editorial Planeta SAIC**
Textos: Vera Giaconi
Investigación: Stella Fernández
Fotografía: Gabriel Domenichelli
Ecónoma: Marcela Sorondo
Producción: Dina Ricci

© 2004, Emecé Editores S. A.
   Independencia 1668, C1100 ABQ,
   Buenos Aires, Argentina
   www.editorialplaneta.com.ar

Arte de cubierta: *Mario Blanco*

1ª edición: octubre de 2004
Impreso en Latingráfica
Impresos Offset,
Rocamora 4161, Capital Federal,
en el mes de octubre de 2004.

IMPRESO EN LA ARGENTINA /
PRINTED IN ARGENTINA
Queda hecho el depósito
que previene la ley 11.723
ISBN· 950-04-2587-4

For the record | 5 |
Historical Background | 6 |
Characteristics of a good barbecue | 8 |
Argentine cuts | 10 |
Meat Cuts | 12 |
Where and how to choose the meat | 14 |
Shopping | 16 |

Troy is burning | 18 |
Grill, wood or coal | 20 |
How to light the fire | 22 |
The science of fire | 23 |
Knives and other accessories | 24 |
Basic characteristics of a good barbecue cook | 26 |

Ladies and gentlemen: the barbecue | 28 |
When to salt the meat | 30 |
Let's get started: cooking | 31 |
ABC of the best barbecue | 32 |
Basic rules | 33 |
Juicy meat, cooked and tender | 34 |
What, when, how: a barbecue chronology | 36 |
Barbecued Tira de Asado | 38 |
Barbecued Steaks | 40 |
Barbecued Vacío and Tapa de asado | 42 |
Barbecued "matambre" | 44 |
Barbecued lomo and colita de cuadril | 45 |

Classics and exceptional | 46 |
Barbecued "achuras" | 48 |
Barbecued sausages | 49 |
Barbecued chicken | 50 |
Barbecued white salmon | 51 |
Barbecued "dorado" | 52 |

Barbecue "on the cross" | 54 |
Barbecue on the cross | 56 |
Lamb on the cross | 58 |
Piglet on the cross | 60 |
Goat on the cross | 61 |

In Good Company | 62 |
A Vegetarian Barbecue | 64 |
Chimichurri: the Argentine sauce | 66 |
"Criolla" sauce, typical and tasty | 67 |
Green Sauce and Walnut Sauce | 68 |
Barbecued Cheese | 69 |
Empanadas (meat pies) from Salta Province | 70 |
Picadita" (hors d'oeuvres) and Empanadas | 71 |
Salads | 72 |
Wine | 74 |
Mate | 76 |
Mate: Bitter or "cimarrón" | 78 |

Acknowledgments

Carlos Grossi, private collection
Antigüedades Ricci
L'Interdit. Arenales 1412
Federación Argentina de Box
Artesanías Argentinas. Montevideo 1307
Champagne. Arenales 1307
La Ferme. Talcahuano 1157
Arandu. Paraguay 1259
Antigua Casa Núñez
Juan Carlos Pallarols. Defensa 1039/94

For the record

W hen it comes to barbecue, it is useless to sit down to consider its origins and ancestry. At the dawn of humanity men placed the flesh of their kill on the fire and admired the results. On this side of the ocean and below the Equator, the first historic barbecue was the one that had the Charrúa Indians as chefs and Juan Díaz de Solís and his sailors as the main dish. Sitting around the fire, for centuries as well as today, gauchos and country folk have cooked kilos upon kilos of beef, pork, mutton, choiques, ñandúes, armadillos, llamas, guanacos and God knows what other creature that just because it walked – as gaucho Martín Fierro put it – ended up on the grill. However, talking of barbecue as gastronomical symbol and marker of the Argentine idiosyncrasy is much more than talking about meat slowly cooking above the embers' heat. It means talking about both science and elemental secrets in order that, once facing the fire, we pay tribute to our national identity. Even though when it comes to barbecues all Argentinians claim to be experts, there are indeed very few, once the table is set, who deserve the traditional applause. Read our recommendations closely, put them consciously into practice, and then, for sure, enjoy the glory.

Historical Background

From the time when travelers of the world exhausted the pampas in order to study and be scandalized by the habits of our gauchos and natives, barbecue and red meat were the basis of the Argentine diet and idiosyncrasy. Charles Darwin, the Robertson brothers, William McCann, Thomas Falkner and many others were amazed or scared when realizing that gauchos could not only butcher whole animals with just their knives, but also travel extraordinary distances without getting tired – all thanks to red meat (and to mate, to a certain extent). In those days, barbecue and "barbecue with the hide," were almost the only options. Entrails were discarded, they made no distinction between different cuts, and grills only arrived on the scene well into the XIX century. Still, even when the gauchos cooked their meat without even skinning it, sat on animal skulls around the fire, ate the steaming, almost raw meat immediately after removing it from the fire using just their knives, our barbecue was already beginning to be renowned in gastronomical circles around the world, at least if we judge by one of Charles Darwin's many comments on the matter: *"If a proper nobleman could have dined with us that night, needless to say that meat barbecued with its hide would have been, very soon, celebrated in London."*

Truth is that in those years, cattle roamed freely in great numbers all over the pampas, the export of hides reached astronomical numbers, and both land and animals knew nothing of "private property." It was then when the gauchos became experts on the art of organizing savage expeditions to hunt down cattle – called "vaquerías" – and on the science of taking advantage of what the exporters rejected: the meat.

▲ "Of how the Indians lasso the horned stock". Florian Paucke, *Through Here and There (A stay among the Mocobi Indians).*

Characteristics of a good barbecue

T he barbecue is not just a gastronomical habit, but also a ceremony that is celebrated using any available excuse: a night spent with friends, the visit of a distant relative, a professional success, a wedding or engagement. In the summer, the night skies in the country, in small towns and in big cities are filled with slender smoke columns – testimony to meetings, animated conversation, wine, and certain abundance. Friends and family, if they know what they are doing, will not approach the cook's grill with cooking advice or reprimands. To deserve such courtesy and not betray the Argentine barbecue mystique, it's important that you not forget certain fundamental details. A barbecue according to God's dictates must have a variety of entrails, Spanish sausages, blood sausages or grilled "salchichas" (Creole sausages) such classic cuts as "matambre" (flank steak), "tira de asado" (short ribs, bone in) "vacío" (thin flank) and a piece of "lomo" (tenderloin) or "tapa de asado" (short ribs, boneless). You might encounter some criticism, even then. So consider adding some vegetables cooked over the embers as well, some grilled cheese and for the fanatics who despise red meat: chicken. The important thing, once clear on the importance of variety, is that before placing the meat on the grill, it must be at room temperature (not frozen or semi-frozen), and whatever happens or whoever may show up, the food must always arrive hot at the table and in the order selected by your eating guests.

Argentine cuts

The gaucho lacks fruits and vegetables; surrounded by cattle, he's often without milk; he lives without bread and has no other food but meat and water.

F. B. HEAD, THE PAMPAS AND THE ANDES

Although once in the butcher shop you won't be able to choose the breed of the animal that will provide the tira de asado (short ribs, bone in) or vacío (thin flank) that you'll put on the grill, it is useful to know the origin of some of the breeds that have made Argentine meat one of the marvels of world cuisine. Of course, there will be detractors and experts who are determined to question the following selection, but these three breeds represent the best:

ABERDEEN ANGUS ▲

This breed originated in the Northeast of Scotland, and was first imported to our country in 1879. Because it is without horns, it is commonly known as the "Stunted Black." Its adaptability to our pampas has made it the most common breed on Argentine ranches. The Aberdeen Angus provides the quality meat that distinguishes Argentine products.

HEREFORD ▶

Originated in England, it was imported to our country in 1862. It is widely distributed among all our cattle lands. One of its main virtues is that it provides the famous "baby beef," a cut up to 10 centimeters thick, highly esteemed both by the international restaurants trade, and by the tourists who visit us, armed with knives and forks.

SHORTHORN ◀

This breed originated in the Northeast of England where it was known under the name Durham. It was the first to be used to improve the local breeds. In 1823 the first bull was imported. Until the beginnings of the 20th century, when it was replaced by the Holland-Argentine breed, most of the milk produced in Argentina was provided by Shorthorn animals. Currently, it is the breed that makes Argentine meat famous all over the world, particularly its young calves.

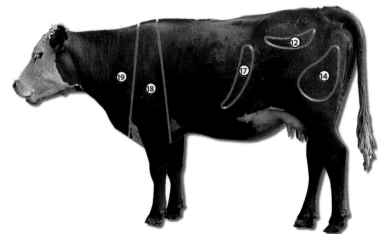

1 Cuadril	5a Bifes Anchos	9 Falda	14 Nalga	19 Cogote
2 Palomita	5b Bifes angostos	10 Azotillo	15 Hueso sin carne	
3a Carnaza de Paleta	6 Aguja	11 Peceto	16 Hueso con carne	
3b Carnaza de cola	7 Matambre	12 Lomo	17 EntraÒa	
4 Bola de lomo	8 Asado	13 Vacio	18 Pecho	

Meat Cuts

The opinion of most travelers, while not negative, was critical of the overwhelming presence of meat. However, those critics did not take into consideration that the country of reference (Argentina), was by definition a producer of meat and not so much a producer of vegetables.

ANDRÉS CARRETERO, DAILY LIFE IN BUENOS AIRES

I n order for you not to look like an amateur in front of your butcher, you need to be familiar with certain fundamentals regarding the most traditional and preferred cuts when the time comes to light up the fire.

STEAKS
El "bife de chorizo" (fore rib, boneless) is located on the external side of the tenderloin. When it comes to "bifes de costilla" (fore rib, bone in) we must take into account a crucial distinction, "bife angosto" (strip loin, bone in) is cut from the back of the animal, and "bife ancho" (fore rib, bone in) from the front. Both kinds of strip are also found on the ribcage inside muscle, but unlike "bife de chorizo" they come attached to the bone.

VACÍO (THIN FLANK)
It is a muscle located on the side of the animal's hindquarters, between the ribs and the hip. The membrane covering it is left on the cut. It is very fibrous meat and very juicy, unmatched characteristics that make it deserving of a privileged position on the grill.

MATAMBRE (FLANK STEAK)
It is the thin and lean meat between the ribs and the hide. It is a typical Argentine cut.

TIRA DE ASADO (SHORT RIBS, BONE IN)
It is the ribcage cut in strips perpendicular to the bones. Even though everybody knows what they look like once they are cooked and on the plate, not everybody knows that it is one of the cuts originated on the most superficial part of the animal and that it is important, which ribs it comes from. Most people prefer the first ribs, because they have less fat and are more flavorful. From the fourth rib till the end, they are greasier and thicker.

TAPA DE ASADO (SHORT RIBS, BONELESS)
This cut covers the upper front of the ribcage. The meat is slightly tougher. In earlier times, the "tapa de asado" was cut together with the "costillar" (ribcage).

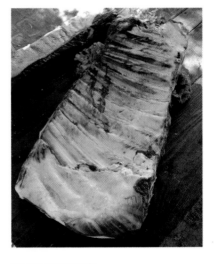

LOMO (TENDERLOIN)
It is a longish cone-shaped muscle. The cut is not without difficulties: it must be perpendicular to the muscle fibers, not horizontal, so it will be sealed by the heat and it won't loose its juices while cooked.

COLITA DE CUADRIL (POINT OF RUMP OR TRIANGLE)
It is a longish cone-shaped muscle cut off the rump. It is important the meat comes from a good animal, or chances are high it will be a tough cut.

COSTILLAR (RIBCAGE)
It is the star of argentine barbecues. It is the cow's ribcage, taken whole to the grill, and not sliced in strips. If your butcher knows what he's doing, the ribcage will be covered with a thin hide-like layer that once cooked and crunchy is a true delicacy.

Where and how to choose the meat

At the en d of each day, they (the gauchos) kill a calf or a fat young bull, and they light a fire with dry grass, bones and the grease and fat of the animal, which is grilled in its entirety, hide and all. This is the only food these men wish, except the mate, which they always take with them.

WILLIAM McCANN,
TWO THOUSAND MILES' RIDE THROUGH THE ARGENTINE PROVINCES

If, as they say, triumph is not obtained on the battlefield, but rather in the maps and the preceding strategy, then, choosing the meat is the indispensable first step to victory on the barbecue. There are several factors to consider. The first is the place where you'll buy the meat.

There are still a few butcher shops where clients are treated as if they were in a hotel. Here, the problem is not the quality of the meat, but its price. For those who want to risk a more excting experience, good meat can be found in any neighborhood butcher shop, provided one evaluates carefully the slaughtered half animal hanging behind the counter. It is simple: the smaller the animal, the tenderer the meat. Those condemned to supermarket aisles, must take into consideration other factors, equally important. First: the smell of the meat and the smell of the fat. Depending on the animal, the flesh tone might go from a pinkish red (in the case of a cow) to a deep red (in the case of a young bull). If that red is darker, veering toward a brownish burgundy, you will be better off considering other options. Regarding the fat, whiter is better. If the fat is yellowish, the meat will likely be tough. In any event, all cuts must have at least a bit of fat to keep their flavor after being barbecued.

If, on top of being condemned to the supermarket, you only have access to those tiny plastic trays, to the foregoing advice we must add one more item: never buy a cut in a carelessly wrapped and bloody container. A

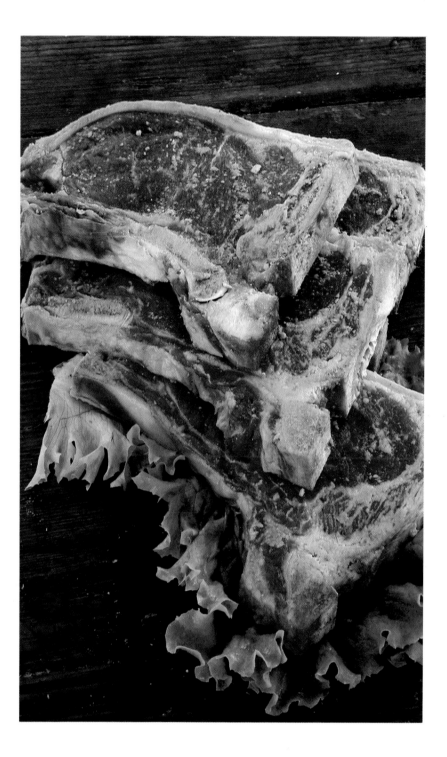

tray in those conditions may hide a dark past. For instance, if it was previously frozen and defrosted, ideally, you should not freeze it again, for in the process, it would have lost all the juices that are a warrant of flavor. With these recommendations committed to memory, we must trust our luck and lead ourselves into temptation.

Shopping

I f you want to enjoy not just the barbecue, but the company, you need to calculate with a certain degree of exactitude the amount of meat and other ingredients (bread, wine, vegetables, etc.) that will be necessary to satisfy all your guests. For that reason, before doing anything else, be certain about the number of people invited to the barbecue. So as not to commit the sin of innocence, add to the initial calculation the number of potential party crashers (boyfriends, recently separated friends, unruly uncles), who are an inevitable fact of life. Once you have a number, in order not to dismiss certain variables, take into account the number of kids, elderly people and women-on-a-diet who will be present, as well as the number of insatiable overeaters, regardless of age and gender. Let's assume that this approximate calculus gives us ten people of average appetite. Figure that, for each of those ten individuals, you'll need half a kilo of meat, so you must buy five kilos of meat. The calculations for "achuras" (entrails) and sausages is separate, keeping in mind that nobody will eat more than one "chorizo" (Spanish sausage) and one "morcilla" (blood sausage), and 250 grams of achuras (entrails). When it comes to bread, allow half a kilo per guest.

As for wine, that is a more delicate matter. Generally speaking, the estimate is 1/2 liter per man and 1/4 liter per woman. But only you know your friends and relatives well enough to know if those numbers are an accurate reflection of their drinking. Regarding salads, traditionally, they are the women's turf. But surely, you'll be in charge of shopping, so know that you must acquire about 100 grams of vegetables per person. If you add to this list such accessories as sodas, water, toothpicks, napkins, ice, barbecue salt, oil and vinegar, it will be unlikely that you'll be caught unawares or that anyone can ruin your party.

Troy is burning

Perhaps you've been lucky enough that your butcher agreed to chop up for you the youngest, pinkest, and most tender cow. Perhaps, next to your barbecue grill you have the most precious collection of meat, entrails and vegetables. Even better, the day may be perfect, the grill need no adjustments and your friends trust your cooking abilities and are willing not to bother you with a single piece of advice. The turning point of any true barbecue cook worth his price will still not have arrived. Perhaps you never thought of it this way; but a good barbecue depends not on the meat, but on the fire, and more specifically, on the embers. Don't think you know everything. Read carefully the following chapter before you get your lighter anywhere near the wood. Or if you do, don't go around telling everybody we didn't warn you.

Grill, wood or coal

Burn in the middle of the country
The fires with bright lights
The wind of the pampas blows
And smoke and sparks fly

ESTEBAN ECHEVERRÍA, LA CAUTIVA

There are many kinds of grills, although here we will only list the most common ones. In cities, you'll find the prefabricated grill, and the grill on wheels. The prefab is built with concrete and the interior is laid out with refracting bricks. They have chimneys (to eliminate the smoke and simultaneously air its interior) and a metal grill of adjustable height with a gutter to collect the grease. They are very practical for those with little experience, because they protect the meat from the cold, the wind, and the rain, and because the distance between the fire and the embers can be regulated without difficulty. They also hold the heat. The grills on wheels are ideal for those who are short on space but still don't want to be deprived of a good barbecue. These grills may have adjustable or removable grids, and such accessories as a furnace, or cover with an air and smoke porthole, to take maximum advantage of the embers' heat. That said, some claim these grills are way too smoky, too small, and that the meat resents the lack of distance between itself and the excessive heat.

For those who have the marvelous advantage of being out in the open, there are country grills: a wire, iron or braided metal grid, either with legs or held up from the floor by bricks or stones. These grills are very cheap and you can build them yourself (with a little ability and a good model) and they also tend to be big, which makes it possible to accommodate the meat without piling up the different cuts. The one disadvantage is that only experienced barbecue cooks can overcome wind, rain, lack of height, and inclement conditions of barbecuing in an open field and come out victorious. Still, it is always worth trying. Last but not least, and for camping and picnic lovers, there are portable grills: a folding metal grid that travels with the barbecue cook as far as his adventurous spirit takes him before hunger forces him to stop.

N owadays supermarkets and other stores offer a wide variety of products that make lighting the fire easier. Among them, the most common ones are:

WOOD	Undoubtedly, wood barbecues are the ones favored by demanding experts. It is easy to purchase bags of dry natural wood. Although wood is difficult to light, it burns better than coal, perfumes the meat, and its embers last longer and stay hotter. Woods from fruit trees produce an aromatic smoke that betters even more the flavor of meat.
VEGETABLE COAL	Chunks of wood without stuffing, burnt through a process that allows them to become coal without being consumed. This coal is available in five or ten kilo bags at supermarkets, gas stations or grocery stores.
BRIQUETTES	A mixture of sawdust, coal and sand, mixed and compacted with a petrol-based substance, these are generally available at supermarkets. They are cleaner than coal and they burn more quickly. Purists argue that they burn too fast and don't perfume the meat. In short, they're very handy, but they're not orthodox.
PINE WOOD	Ideal to start the fire. It is a light wood that burns easily. Get it from vegetable and fruits' cradles.
FIRESTARTER PILLS	Useable without the precautions necessary when using such other inflammables as alcohol or kerosene, these are square blocks of compacted sawdust embedded with gas.

How to light the fire

Before even approaching the podium of the great Argentine barbecue cooks, you must know how to light, and keep fiery till the end, a fire worth its price. For that purpose, the crucial question is: wood or coal? Tradition and most rigorous palates indicate that the fire must be started with wood, because it gives the meat the typical smoky flavor of a "criollo" barbecue. But that's not all there is to it. The cook must tend the wood so it will provide good heat without sparks (which would not only humiliate you in front of an audience, but might also affect the guests directly). Quebracho, algarrobo, and lapacho wood meet the requirements, and also generate long-lasting embers, saving you from guesstimating and last-minute additions (which never work or solve the problems anyway). Now, all that said, if you'd rather use coal, or simply find it easier, go ahead. There are no true gauchos left to avenge the heresy.

Once the wood has been selected you should start the fire in the area of the grill destined to hold the embers (it can be the grill's floor or a metal cradle). Build a small pile of light wood and strips of newspaper. Pile the paper first, and on top of it, crisscross the pieces of wood for faster combustion (wood from vegetable and fruit crates are ideal). Light the paper and wait for the first flames. If you're going to use coal, do the same, replacing the wood with the coal briquettes. When the fire starts to grow before your eyes, don't let your enthusiasm or other distractions blind you, and add, little by little, the harder wood or the coal without overloading the pile, to prevent the fire from being extinguished. Help the fire grow by fanning it with a piece of cardboard, a shovel, a piece of wood, a napkin, or asking your pesky relatives to blow into the fire for several minutes.

For good embers, you need at least half an hour. They are distinguished by their incandescent, reddish color, and are covered by whitish ashes. Don't be discouraged as you wait. Just think how well your efforts will be rewarded: the barbecue cook gets, not merely all the applause at the end, but also is the center of attention beforehand, surrounded by all sorts of compliments and gestures of affection.

The science of fire

Fire is a chemical reaction that involves three elements: heat, combustion and oxygen. If any of these elements is eliminated, the fire will be extinguished. For that reason, once the first flames have risen you must carefully add the wood or coals, because if you add too much, you'll diminish the amount of oxygen and suffocate the combustion. If you need to revive the fire or were about "to drown" it, add oxygen to your equation with the aid of a fan or blowing into the fire. On the grill, the meat must be exposed to a dry heat that dehydrates it and changes the proteins, sugars and fats' structures. For this reason, you'll want to avoid humid wood, not merely because it is more difficult to light and significantly smokier, but also because it exhales a moist vapor that ruins the cooking process and the flavor of the meat.

• **WHEN CHOOSING THE WOOD,** make sure that it is not green or moist. It is not just more difficult to light up (when it is not impossible), it also produces a lot of smoke.

• **THE BEST EMBERS** are those resulting from hard woods, although, you'll see, they are more difficult to light. Please, avoid using kerosene, gasoline, gas oil or any other flammable products: they stink and they considerably alter the flavor of the meat.

• **DON'T PILE UP LIGHT WOOD,** paper and wood or coals in such a manner that they prevent free air circulation.

• **DON'T MAKE BALLS** with the newspaper that you'll use to light up the fire (they burn too fast). Instead, twist the paper into paper sticks.

• **IF YOU'RE GOING TO USE COAL,** make sure it is of good quality, that way you'll prevent fireworks and uncomfortable sparks.

Knives
and other accessories

There are many who will say, "with a knife and a fork I have more than enough," in the belief that they're affirming their position as tried-and-true barbecue cooks. Nonetheless, knowing how to use certain other tools can considerably improve your results.

The knife is the only utensil that's truly indispensable. They come in as many varieties as cooks have preferences, but when it comes to a barbecue, you'd be well advised to get a very sharp knife with a wide and sharply pointed blade. You will also find it useful to have a matched set of long, metal-handled knife and fork (to manipulate the meat over the grill without burning your forearms as a condemned man to the fire). To keep your knives sharp, you can resort to a sharpening stone, an electrical sharpener or a "chaira" (a metal sharpening stick). The only thing that really matters is that the blades are always sharp and cut the meat without making it scream or shredding it.

Your guests, on the other hand, will likely suggest that the most important implements from their viewpoint (other than good teeth) are a good set of knives with sharp, serrated blades, and forks with wooden handles – and they're right.

Handcrefted knives with leather and silver embossed sheathes. ▲

Kitchen knives and sharpening stick ("chaira"). ◄

Horn-hilted knives. ▼

Poker, tongs and shovel. ▶

But the barbecue cook cannot live by knives alone. Other accessories that may turn out to be useful are: a poker (to aerate the embers or break up the bigger ones), and a metal shovel (to move the hot embers from one place to another under the grill).

Keep in mind that it is important that the meat retains its juices all through the cooking process. For that reason, it might be handy to acquire a set of long tongs (the ones with rounded ends, like a spiral) that allow you to flip the meat, or to take it from the grill to the serving tray without having to pierce it.

Another helpful ally is the cutting board. If possible, choose a big board, with gutters near the edges, so you won't lose the meat's juices. You might also find it useful to have a broad brush (like a painter's) to marinate the meat during grilling; a gastronomical syringe to inject liquors or lemon juice into meats and chickens, and a good metal prong (a brochette stick) to use with sausages and entrails, to make your work on the grill easier.

If you're going to barbecue chicken or pork, having a pair of carving scissors will come in handy (a piece of advice: do not make use of pruning or tailor's scissors; much less of those tiny Chinese scissors good only for crafts). If you're going to barbecue fish, make use of metallic presses (they will allow you to flip the fish without damaging the meat). And of course, if you're an honest-to-God barbecue cook, you'll also want a good glass of wine and good company.

Basic characteristics of a good barbecue cook

R ed-faced and slightly roasted, the barbecue cook is the soul of any barbecue ceremony. To the invaluable gesture of waking early – and on many occasions forsaking the comfort of a Sunday bed – the barbecue cook adds the ordeal of suffering the heat more than any of his friends or relatives, and that the smell of smoke, and barbecued meat impregnates his clothing. If by chance, wisdom, or default you find yourself one day facing the responsibility of barbequing, always remember that the grill is your domain. Nobody has the right to argue about the way to place the meat on the grill, nor to expound on his or her own theories about the amount of heat, much less to get a single finger close to the grill and attempt to serve themselves as if they were at an "all-you-can-eat" restaurant. To defend your grill from anxious and irreverent guests, it is not necessary you parade yourself in front of your relatives and friends with the face of Clint Eastwood on a day he's suffering from liver pains. It is enough that you be decisive and give at least the appearance of knowing what you're doing. Decide beforehand which one will be your technique: salting the meat before or after cooking it; placing the strips of meat with the bone against the fire or the other way around; if you will leave the steak half an hour or forty minutes on the grill, and afterwards, defend it with all your might against those who, suffering neither heat nor smoke nor pressure, swear that they're true barbecue philosophers. Keep in mind that when facing the grill you're not just the general, you're also the Foreign Affairs Secretary. Thus, while it is your duty to defend meat and other cuts until they are ready, you must also be the perfect host and

make sure all your guests have their glasses
full, that conversation doesn't decay and that
every single guest gets his choice of meat
done the way he likes it best. After all, artists
must work to collect their audiences'
applause.

Ladies and gentlemen: the barbecue

A re you one of those people who believe that a barbecue is merely cooking meat and entrails on a fire? Do you truly believe the myth that affirms that Argentinian are born with a special instinct that protects us from embarrassment when facing the grill? Is it possible that there are still people who think that with a bit of fire, good meat and a grill, success is at hand? We all need to know some secrets, refresh some techniques, and polish away some vices and caprices if we want to barbecue properly the blessed meat and its relatives.

When to salt the meat

I f the fire debate is between those favoring wood and those favoring coal, where cooking is concerned, the primary question is when to salt the meat: before or after cooking it?

Though much has been said and written on this topic, we're sorry to inform you that there are no absolute truths, so you'll have to make your own decision. The one thing we can offer you is a careful exposition regarding the pros and cons of each position.

Those who favor of salting the meat after cooking (either when it has already been served, or after having placed it on the grill) affirm that that way the meat does not lose its juices (or, as some more properly argue, the salt does not absorb the meat's juices). Those who favor salting the meat before placing it on the grill argue that that way the meat absorbs the salt better, and ends up more flavorful. If you subscribe to this view, you may find it convenient to salt it with coarse salt, and to massage it into the meat so the salt will better penetrate it. Still other folks favor salmuera (salt diluted in water), and dress the meat by brushing it abundantly during cooking.

Keep in mind these descriptions so you can choose the option that best suits your preferences.

Let's get started: cooking

Not much can be guaranteed regarding the amount of heat and the amount of time required for a barbecue. Partly this is because each meat cut, each type of entrails and sausage has its own gastronomical clock and partly because each grill (open, closed, etc.) alters the equation. Still, it's possible to impart some advice that will ease your uncertainty. First and most important, make sure you have embers enough to take you to the finish line. If that is not the case, or if you have doubts, fix the problem while you still have time to do something about it (don't wait till the last moment, when you have half-cooked meat, and interrupting the cooking process will make it unsalvageable). Spread the embers under the grill drawing a mental map telling you which cuts will lie where. Remember, for instance, that thicker cuts will need more embers and more heat, and that "morcillas" (blood sausages) are already cooked and need only to be heated up. Next, make sure that the grill's floor is hot, and only then place the meat on the metal grill. The cooking surface should never be higher than fifteen centimeters from the embers (or when Monday comes you'll still be waiting for the first round of "chinchulines" [intestines]) and never lower than ten centimeters. The basic thing is to obtain a good "seal" in that first moment. This means exposing the meat to a high heat for a couple of minutes so the exterior layer of the meat gets seared, increasing its ability to keep in juices. You can get this result either by lowering the grill or increasing the amount of embers. Everything depends on your ability and the possibilities offered by your grill. After this initial searing, only two questions will torment you: when to flip the meat and how not to ruin everything. For the first issue you need only know that the moment to flip the meat arrives when you start to see the first drops of blood on the upper side of the meat. Once turned over, the same phenomenon will notify you it is time to remove the meat from the grill. Regarding the second issue, a single piece of advice: never retreat, never get distracted.

ABC
of the best barbecue

I f you have read the chapter about cooking with some attention, you are already familiar with some of the basic aspects wich pave the long way to an unforgettable barbeque. However, and even though certain pieces of knowledge can only be attained through experience, this section provides ten golden rules to achieve the best barbecue and to avoid certain sins which every careless barbecue cook is tempted to commit.

Basic rules

ONE	Although, like any other barbecue cook, you must also be the host, don't let yourself be tempted by conversation and other distractions. Do not forget that a true cook always has one eye set on the party's progress (that is: his guests' glasses) and the other on the grill.
TWO	Before laying down the meat, the grill must be clean, without grease, soot, or ashes. Once everything is very hot, rub it with a piece of fat.
THREE	You must control the intensity of the fire from the very beginning all the way to the end of the cooking process, paying attention to the particular needs of each of the ingredients on your grill.
FOUR	So as not to interrupt the cooking process, giving the meat a boiled-like flavor, it is crucial that you correctly estimate the amount of embers you'll need
FIVE	The meat, the cheese, the entrails and sausages must not be frozen or semi-frozen when you place them on the grill (so they don't end up raw inside). If necessary, leave them outside the refrigerator until they reach room temperature.
SIX	The meat must not be moved around on the grill. A chef worth his name moves the embers (to distribute the heat correctly) not the meat. Besides, the cuts he offers present those tempting golden lines, witnesses of the time spent on the grill (those lines are impossible to obtain if the steaks wander all around the grill).
SEVEN	After the initial "sealing," the meat is flipped only once, without puncturing it (so it won't lose its juices), with the aid of metal tongs or a similar utensil.
EIGHT	Don't ever cut into the meat to check "how things are going." The pieces of meat must reach your guests' plates intact and with all their juices.
NINE	The barbecue must be offered very hot and just off the grill.
TEN	Wine is your best ally, but it can also become your worst enemy. Drink in moderation until all your guests have been served or leave your knives with a trusted relative.

Juicy meat, cooked and tender

€ ach guest has his preferences, and it is the duty of a good cook and a better host to take every preference into consideration when offering the different cuts. Never complaining and always smiling, be aware that the difference between a well done, a rare and a medium-rare piece of meat depends on attention and dexterity alone. Let's examine the fundamental differences so we won't be ruled by first impressions.

• VERY RARE

Only for the brave. The meat is barely singed and ends up semi-raw and very red inside.

• RARE OR JUICY

The meat acquires a light brown color on the outside and is pink inside and very juicy. Warning: not to be confused with the very rare variety, which looks almost red.

• MEDIUM

The cook must pay attention and flip the meat or remove it from the grill as soon as he sees the red dots of juice on the upper side. The meat will be brown outside, and its interior will be slightly drier than a juicy cut.

• WELL DONE

The meat will be dark brown outside, light brown inside and leaning towards dry or with brown juices. Important: do not confuse meat well done with meat overdone, which resembles shoe leather.

COOKING POINT "MEDIUM"

Warning

Among the many crimes committed in front of a grill, some are simply unjustifiable. Others will make your time at the grill truly shameful. Worst of all, the evidence will be unavoidable and the corpus delicti will expose what can only be called a:

• RUSHED BARBECUE

The accused surely succumbed to pressure or hurry, didn't know how to control the heat or forgot to place the grill at least 10 centimeters high. The meat is burnt outside and raw inside (raw, not juicy, as the accused will claim).

• SPASM-ED OR COOLED BARBECUE

The worst possible crime: Left with too few embers, or, trying to accommodate some inconsiderate guests who arrived late, the accused has let the meat cool during the cooking process to "slow it down." The meat will look perfect on the outside, but appearances are deceiving: inside it will be raw and bloody.

• STEWED OR BOILED BARBECUE

Evidently, the accused was thinking about something else or confused the time required by a grilled barbecue with that of a barbecue "on the cross [the U.S. word is "spit"]." The meat was exposed to a mild heat for endless hours and resembles a stew: soft, without juices and with the fibers destroyed.

• RAW BARBECUE

Distracted, anxious or lacking judgment, the cook removed the meat from the grill before its time. The meat is beige on the outside and bloody red inside. It can, in a pinch, be returned to the grill, but the punishment fits the crime: the barbecue will not be perfect.

• OVERCOOKED BARBECUE

Whether because he was attending to some guests, or simply didn't pay enough attention, the meat has been exposed to heat for far too much time, and looks like the sole of a shoe: without shine, without juices and almost black on the outside. The verdict: its flavor has been definitively altered.

What, when, how: a barbecue chronology

The order in which ingredients reach the pot can be crucial for the outcome of a stew, and in much the same way, it's important that you follow a certain chronology if you want your barbecue to be an example of harmony in which everybody ends up satisfied. A wood fire **takes up to one hour** before it produces good embers. Coals take about thirty minutes. Depending on how you want to wait for your guests (with the barbecue already on the table, or still in your pajamas), plan as follows.

Once the embers are ready and the grill hot, your first step should be to start cooking the "chorizos" (Spanish sausages), "riñones" (kidneys) and "mollejas" (sweetbreads) (also the vegetables, if you're thinking about including them).

Fifteen minutes later, it will be the time for the "chinchulines" (intestines), and if it is in your plan, the chicken.

Another fifteen minutes later it is time for the "salchichas parrilleras" (Creole sausages), "tira de asado"

(short ribs, bone in), the provoleta cheese and the "morcillas" (blood sausages) (keep in mind you only have to heat them up).

Yet another fifteen minutes, and you'll lay down the "lomo" (tenderloin) or "colita de cuadril" (point of rump or triangle), the "vacío" (thin flank) and the steaks. By this time the "chorizos" (Spanish sausages), the "salchichas parrilleras" (Creole sausages) and the "morcillas" (blood sausages) will be ready for the table. Don't get distracted, though, because only **in another fifteen** minutes will it be time to put the matambre (flank steak) on the grill, and the tapa de asado (short ribs, boneless) and to start serving the "chinchulines" (intestines), "mollejas" (sweetbread) and "riñones" (kidneys). The sound of forks and mandibles, by now, should be deafening, but nobody will forget to give thanks when it's time for you to offer "asado de tira" (short ribs, bone in) and the other meat cuts cooked as requested by each guest – and then, finally, **applause for the cook!**

Barbecued Tira de Asado (Short ribs, bone in)

For a traditional Argentine barbecue, certain cuts are unavoidable. Among them, and perhaps occupying the first place on the marquee, is the "tira de asado" (short ribs, bone in) or the "costillar" (ribcage) -- indisputably Argentine cuts. It is an accepted fact that the thicker the strip of ribs, the wiser the cook; and the thinner, the more hurried he is to get rid of his guests (you might have noticed this on commercial grills and restaurants). Once you have enough embers and your grill is very hot and clean, it is crucial that as with any other cut with bones, you first place the strip with the bones towards the embers. The strip will be flipped only once, to give a golden finish to the meaty side. Do not wander around with the meat all over the grill, do not stab it too often, and do not cut it to see "how it's doing." Only if the cut is very thick can you turn it to have each of its four sides resting on the grill. And only if you are in a hurry (or don't have good butcher friends who've saved you a decent piece of meat) and the strips you've got are too thin, can you cook it first on the meaty side. When it comes to salt, it is important to be generous with the short ribs. They have so much fat that melts with the heat, and the salt gets washed away with it.

Barbecued Steaks

A although it is hard to believe, as tourists enthusiastic at the prospect of eating a typical Argentine steak crowd thousands of restaurants, it's only fair to acknowledge our barbecue has a foreign origin. Suffice it to say that the word "bife" comes from the English "beef steak," which merely means "slice of meat."

The "bife de chorizo" (boneless fore rib), generally arrives at the table without any dressing other than salt (except that – as many prefer – the salt is left for after the cooking) and with a bit of fat on one side that helps to hold the flavor of the meat. To avoid curling during the cooking, you can slice the nerve that surrounds the cut. Some folks prefer steaks "butterfly style" that is, sliced lengthwise through the middle and open like a book. Cooking time depends, always, on the cook's intuition, but it is also determined by the steak's thickness and guests' preferences as to doneness. It's important to use tongs (not a fork, as puncturing the cut will make it lose its juices), and flip the steak only once to ensure several parallel stripes on each side, a sure signal of its time on the grill. Beyond taste and preferences, it is no secret that among those who choose a "bife de chorizo," most prefer it "medium rare," and those who choose a "bife de costilla" (same cut, with the bone) prefer it "well done."

Barbecued Vacío (thin flank) and Tapa de asado (boneless short ribs)

Looking back at the history of barbecue, it's clear that while the gauchos may have known a lot about the slaughtering of the animal, they were no experts when it came to choosing which parts of it to place on the grill (the entrails and the organs were unanimously discarded). Nowadays, with the gauchos' habits having extended to all Argentine tables, which cut to choose, how to gauge its quality, and how to grill it, are all subject to debate. And on Sundays, each and every one of the people around the table – all expert, of course – shows off his or her own traditions and secrets.

It's the middle parts of the animals that are most commonly used -- such as "tira de asado" (short ribs, bone in), "tapa de asado" (boneless short ribs) and "vacío" (thin flank). As with other, thinner cuts (such as "matambre" [extremely thin flank steak]) it is useful to place both "vacío" and "tapa de asado" on the grill at the very end, after the "tira de asado," the organ meat and the sausages. Do not remove the fat and the membrane from the "vacío" (a true delicacy once it's cooked golden and crunchy), just make some cuts on it so it won't curl up on itself while cooking. Once on the grill, the meat must be flipped only once halfway through the cooking process (get a good pair of tongs so you can flip it without destroying it with forks and knives). Of course you can marinate it with "chimichurri" (barbecue sauce) while cooking it, but if the meat is of good quality, the best thing is to give it ample room to shine on its own. Before serving, and for those who prefer their meat golden brown, you can lower the grill a bit closer to the embers, for a last blast of heat.

If your guests know what they're doing, and you managed to get through the intricacies of the vacío (thin flank)'s cooking process, it needs no more company than a good glass of red wine, and a knife and fork.

Barbcued "matambre" (flank steak)

I want to be the medium of modest apologies, and in the same way other people write about the life of illustrious men, I want to transmit, if possible, to the remotest posterity, the true historical encomium endlessly taking place with each chewing jaw, each tooth crashing, each palate savoring, the juicy and most illustrious "matambre."

ESTEBAN ECHEVERRÍA, MATAMBRE'S APOLOGY

Matambre (flank steak) occupies a privileged position in Argentine cuisine, whether it is prepared rolled up with vegetables, or with milk, or pizza-like, or even as a component in the stuffing of some of the empanadas from the North of the country. To tenderize it before cooking, some prefer to submerge it in hot milk and let it marinate for several hours – an unnecessary process if the cut is already tender. On the grill, you must place it whole, with its fat and its "cuerito" (membrane). If the matambre is too skinny and fatless, place it with the fatty side up and flip it only at the very end, for a final blast of heat. If it is thick, do the opposite: place the fat towards the fire, flipping only at the end, for the final touch. There are those who prefer to fold the matambre in half, leaving the fatty layer on the outside; in that case, once both sides have turned golden brown, unfold the matambre, and place the inward side towards the fire. An Argentine invention, this delicate meat membrane, matambre, that allows for infinite variations on the "criolla" cuisine, is a dish that not only "kills hunger" (as its Spanish name unequivocally indicates), but when properly handled on the grill, becomes one of the prime delicacies of that national ceremony called barbecue.

Barbcued lomo (tenderloin) and colita de cuadril (point of rump)

Like haute cuisine, barbecues inspire gourmands of sophisticated, subtle and elegant taste. These demanding folks will no doubt agree that only two cuts -- "lomo" (tenderloin) and "colita de cuadril" (point of rump) -- are up to their caprice. Both are among the most tender and expensive cuts available, and currently, they are preferred in modern grill restaurants where nothing smells like anything and where nearly-adolescent waitresses treat customers the way they treat their parents: with utter contempt. First, you should know that the "lomo" has its humor. The cut may be very good or even very expensive, but if cut improperly, it will amount to nothing. Control your friendly butcher and don't be distracted by conversation: the cut must be perpendicular to the muscle fibers, not horizontal, so the heat will seal it and the juices won't be lost during the grilling. When it comes to "colita de cuadril" it is vital that the cut originates in a good animal, or you face high chances that it will be tough.

Then, with lomo (tenderloin), you need to decide if you're going to cook it whole, open in the middle "mariposa" (butterfly) style (to accelerate the cooking process), or in thick slices. Keep in mind that both the "colita de cuadril" (point of rump) and the "lomo" (tenderloin) are longish conical shaped muscles, so the best approach will be to pile up embers under the thicker part of the cut so the grilling will be even. When it comes to salting the meat, be generous, to bring out the flavor.

Classic and exceptional

Nobody can dispute the preferential place that organ meat and sausages occupy in Argentine barbecues. Chicken and fish are still fighting for a place in the spotlight and depend on good techniques and proven recipes for us to contribute to their struggle and bring them nearer a much deserved acknowledgment. In the following pages you'll find a detailed guide and some advice so that your "chinchulines" (intestines), "mollejas" (sweetbreads), "chorizos" (Spanish sausages), "pechugas" (chicken breasts), and "dorados" (a variety of fresh water fish) will garner cheers and applause when they reach the table.

Barbecued "achuras" (organ meat)

W hen gaucho Martín Fierro was still traveling the pampas, the barbecue ritual was a bit different from what we know now. Indians and gauchos, for instance, did not take advantage of the animals' entrails, though it is difficult today to imagine them wasting such delicacies. They gave us the word "achuras" (or "achuraj") meaning, "that which is no good" or "that which is waste."

• MOLLEJA (SWEETBREADS)

These are glands found only in young animals. Always choose heart sweetbreads, since they are less greasy than those from around the neck. Many folks choose to tenderize them with a blast of steam to remove the fat and the tissue enveloping them, others prefer to marinate them in warm milk or macerate them with brandy and laurel leaves. If the "molleja" is large, you can split it in halves (placing the inside towards the fire), or cook it and then cut it in slices about 1 cm thick. Cooking time is approximately 40 minutes. They're best when golden in color and hot, perhaps sprinkled with a bit of lemon juice.

• CHINCHULINES (INTESTINES)

They must first be marinated in water (or milk, for several hours), and washed well before being placed on the grill. Some chefs remove the fat and braid the chinchulines, although most people prefer to cut them in small wheels for individual servings. In any event, they must spend thirty to fifty minutes over the fire, and as with "mollejas," it is considered almost a crime not to serve them well done and crunchy.

• RIÑONES (KIDNEYS)

These require the same treatment as above – marinating -- to eliminate bitter memories of their organ function. The first step is to remove the fat and the skin covering them. Afterwards, you can let them sit overnight in vinegar and coarse salt, or you can let them rest for several hours in red wine. On the grill, they are placed whole, sliced in half, or in 1 cm-thick slices. They must be cooked over a gentle fire, for about forty minutes to an hour.

Barbecued sausages

By definition, sausages are those preparations based on fat and ground meat stuffed inside animal tripe or membranes. Meat can be either pork or beef, but the sausages ruling the Argentine grills are three: "chorizo" (Spanish sausage), "morcilla" (blood sausage) and "salchicha parrillera" (Creole sausage).

• MORCILLA (BLOOD SAUSAGE)

Its stuffing is based on blood and bits of pork. Once the stuffing is made, it is cooked and then wrapped in tripe. As a result, "morcillas" only need to be re-heated over the fire. You will find several options at Argentine butchers: blood sausages with walnuts, sweet, with green onions, Basque (with raisins), and others.

• CHORIZO (SPANISH SAUSAGE)

King of kings, the "chorizo" is deserving of a shopper's most tender care. Do not be satisfied with your closest butcher, rather, go to your most trusted one. You won't want to become a victim of past-their-prime meats, or coloring or indefinable ingredients. If you can choose, don't be shy and go for "chorizos" (sausages) well seasoned with hot peppers and red pepper. If, when mixed, the "chorizos" had too much water or grease, they may explode during grilling. To avoid disaster, place the "chorizos" in cold water for about five minutes before placing them on the grill (that way you'll soften the tripe wrapping them, and they will be better able to withstand the push of boiling water inside). They must be cooked over a gentle fire for about forty minutes. Some folks place the chorizos on a brochette, to flip them more easily, other folks, more puritans, won't ever puncture them, and only flip them with tongs. Most people -- and this is way beyond arguing – prefer to eat them in the unmatchable companionship of an open baguette.

• SALCHICHA PARRILLERA (CREOLE SAUSAGE)

Very similar to the "chorizo" as far as stuffing and cooking method goes, the only caveat regarding the "salchicha parrillera" (Creole sausage) is that it is best to wrap it on itself in a spiral before placing it on the grill and to cook it for no more than twenty minutes or until it is golden on both sides.

Barbecued chicken

For those tired of red meat, or those among your guests who are dieting or whose cholesterol levels have passed the roof, the barbecued chicken is a five-star option. The first step is to choose a memorable bird. A chicken of about two kilos, not big boned, but with breasts deserving of a photo and applause. You should open the chicken by the belly (making an incision on each side of the entrails' cavity), to flatten, empty and wash it well. Place it on the grill with the breast facing up and the belly cavity facing the embers and only when it has reached a truly golden color on that side should you flip it. Cooking may last about an hour, and you should keep an eye out so the heat will be intense and constant. Some people prefer their chicken unseasoned. Other folks prefer to brush it with a simple mixture of oil, garlic and parsley, or to wash or inject it with lemon juice, whisky or brandy. The important thing is: chicken meat should not be juicy, it should be well done, with its skin golden and crunchy.

Barbecued white salmon

We owe the presence of salmon and trout in our waters to Perito Francisco Moreno. But to whom do we owe the presence of the marvelous salmon on our plates and grills? That's a question without an answer. Let's swim in the uncertainty toward this simply-cooked dish, which however has a certain science to it, and await the moment of serving, which will add charm to this privileged creature of Patagonic lakes and rivers.

Although it is common to barbecue fish wrapped in aluminum foil, especially to avoid its skin sticking to the grill's bars, with salmon, we suggest cooking it directly over the grill or on a wire mesh, so the meat is not deprived of the fire's aroma and a light smoky flavor. You can also burn alongside, a fresh twig of rosemary or eucalyptus, to improve the smoky flavor even further. Before placing it on the grill, you'll want to define the flavor of the meat by seasoning the slices of white salmon with salt and pepper (to taste) and pouring some lemon and orange juice on them, and letting them sit on a tray in the refrigerator for about an hour. With the embers providing a medium temperature, and the grill's bars very clean, place the slices over the fire. When they are golden on one side, flip them carefully so the meat won't break and finish the cooking. The meat is well done when the fork enters and exits it with ease. Fish must be cooked through, but not overcooked, or it will end up too dry. Always control the embers' temperature and don't be distracted when the time comes to remove it from the fire.

Serve with a flourish –a dash of butter mixed with parsley, herbs, salt and pepper.

INGREDIENTS FOR FOUR SERVINGS:

WHITE SALMON, 4 SLICES

| SALT AND PEPPER, TO TASTE

| JUICE OF 1 ORANGE AND 1 LEMON

| BUTTER, room temperature, 150 GRAMS

| PARSLEY, minced, 2 TABLESPOONS

| HERBS, fresh, minced, 2 TABLESPOONS

(oregano, thyme, salve, or whichever you like)

Barbecued "dorado"

The dorado is a unique species. Its meat is always exquisite, it appearance beautiful and – as if all that were not enough – for those who favor sport fishing, it is a true challenge. It is not a coincidence that its other name is "river tiger." Its body is wide and strong (some animals weigh over twenty kilograms and are more than 90 cm. long) and during periods of migration a fish can travel over 500 km. Be aware of all this before firing up the grill, and show some respect for the animal you're about to split open and stuff with vegetables and condiments.

After the reverence, and with the fish already cleaned, stuff it with sliced onions, peppers' strips and filleted garlic. Season it with salt, pepper and ground peppers. Very carefully, place the fish on the wire press and place it over the grill on a slow fire of evenly distributed embers. Like any other big animal, it must take its time on the heat so as not to lose its qualities. Fish must be grilled on one side first, and flipped only once. How do you know when it is ready? When pressing the flesh with a fork, the meat separates easily. Fish should not be overcooked, because the flesh dries up and loses its original flavor.

To go with it, offer a strong and muscular red wine, such as Cabernet Sauvignon; it will be marvelous with the fatty and tasty meat of this giant.

INGREDIENTS FOR FIVE OR MORE SERVINGS: **DORADO,** middle size, approximately five kilos, **1**
| **PEPPERS, ENOUGH FOR STUFFING** | **ONION, ENOUGH FOR STUFFING**
| **GARLIC CLOVES,** filleted, **ENOUGH FOR STUFFING** | **SALT, TO TASTE** | **PEPPER, TO TASTE**
| **GROUND PEPPER, TO TASTE**

Barbecue "on the cross" (on the spit)

Before the mid-19th century, when grills were invented –say, the period between the 16th and 19th centuries– meat was barbecued whole, stabbed on wood or metal rods planted in the ground to face the fire. This traditional means of cooking meat – evolved somewhat– still exists today, and there are those who swear that no grilled meat can come close to the beef, piglet or lamb on the cross. Even tourists cannot avoid the temptation when the meat seems to be waiting for them with open arms in the windows of local grills, dripping their juices by the heat of a good fire. Like any other technique, spit-grilling has its secrets, and this chapter will abound in advice and suggestions to help you pay tribute to our cross.

Barbecue
on the cross

Although some people are convinced it's just a question of accessories, what really differentiates a grilled barbecue from one on the cross is that on the latter, the fire is much more important than the embers. The quality of the wood, its hardness, and the intensity of the heat produced by it will be the key to your success. It is important not to get distracted with minor issues such as the "picada" (hors d'oeuvres), or having your guests' glasses always full and be always attentive to the fire's humor. Feed it when it looks sad and control it so that it smokes the meat, and not your party.

Barbecuing on the cross offers two options: with a single fire, or with a fire shaped like a circle around the cross. The first is perhaps the more traditional method, with the cross leaning towards the fire, which must be intense. In the second method, the fire surrounds the cross at a distance of about half a meter. In either case –and without exception– the fire must be provided by such hard woods as "algarrobo" or "quebracho" (local varieties), because their caloric concentration is higher and their embers last longer.

Lamb on the cross

Lamb is emblematic of Patagonia and Tierra del Fuego, as its first animals owed their care to the English and Wales immigrants established in the area. Sheep from the Argentine south are worthy of an anthology of their own. Naturally fed on hard Patagonic grass and without special grains, its meat is so delicious that it can replace beef in any dish (no matter how upsetting this might be to northern Pampeanos). Although it's not easy to find, on the national market, meat of a comparable quality to what's exported, it is worth trying. And if you have acquired a whole lamb, freshly slaughtered, what better way to celebrate than to place it on the cross and give it four or five hours in front of the fire while you entertain your guests. First thing, remove the head and open the rest of the animal down the center of its chest and stomach with a cut from the rectum to the neck. Press on the back to flatten. Tie it to the cross with thick wire, so it won't slip during the grilling. Then plant the cross in the ground with the ribs facing the fire and, as we've said before, make sure the flames are intense and constant. Once the ribcage is done, you must turn it around so the back gets cooked, too. Your efforts will deservedly be rewarded with applause, not just as a courtesy or pity, provided that the lamb arrives on the table hot and crunchy.

Piglet on the cross

I f you trust your butcher, you may want to ask about the origins of the victim. The best piglets are those from the country, organically fed. With a four to five kilogram piglet you'll have enough to feed at least eight very hungry guests.

First thing, before taking it anywhere near the fire, clean the piglet and disassemble the ribcage to open it. Second, place it on a tray, covered with "criolla" sauce and let it spend its last night whole, marinating. Next morning, you'll place the piglet on the cross, with the head down and the hind legs well tied to the cross with wire, so it won't slip while cooking. When the fire is ready, plant the cross in the ground with the piglet's ribs facing the fire and leaning slightly forward. Keep the wind's direction in mind, so the meat doesn't get completely smoked. During the cooking, you can keep dressing the meat with "criolla" sauce. Some people are not good at calculations and misjudge the amount of embers they'll need to finish the barbecue adequately. If you think that might be the case, start another fire that will allow you to keep adding embers whenever you need to. Important: do not move the cross and do not turn it around until, four or five hours later, the ribs have acquired a golden color and the hide, when poked, is crunchy (if it makes noise, the wait is over).

Goat on the cross

Nursing goats, also known as "chivitos" or "cabritos," are usually castrated animals of four months of age or younger. Their meat is tender and much more delicate than lamb. Although not as traditional as other pieces, such as beef ribcage or lamb, "cabrito" is a delicacy deserving of all of our attention. Before doing anything else, make sure your buy has been "aerated." If it has, remove its head, and open the animal's ribcage and stomach by slicing from the rectum to the neck, pressing in its back to flatten it (if you are easily impressionable, you can ask your butcher to do the honors). On the cross, place it with its ribs facing the fire, and be aware that the fire must be intense and constant. Always paying attention to the flames, let time and conversation flow slowly, because the "cabrito" won't be ready for the table for at least four or five hours. Some folks prefer dressing the "cabrito" with "chimichurri" a few hours prior to the barbecue, others choose to offer the sauces only when the table is ready and the forks have assumed the "attack" position. Select, for this tender flesh of delicate yet well defined flavor, a young red wine, with adequate vitality and acidity so it won't dispute the marquee or try to take over the starring role.

In Good Company

A barbecue is a barbecue, but as with any other ceremony, it has its preambles, a courtship period and accompaniments. Salads, wine, mate, "empanadas" (meat pies) and such sauces as "chimichurri" or "criolla" are well deserving of their own. In the following pages you will find everything necessary for the meat to reach the table with the best companions, so that even your most demanding guests will not feel betrayed by the details that make Sunday barbecues, a truly national celebration.

A Vegetarian Barbecue

S ome Argentine barbecue cooks and traditionalists will consider this a heresy, but what actual arguments are there for not letting vegetables reach the grill? Thanks to those less orthodox and more imaginative spirits, for some years now, barbecued vegetables have increased in their variety and the results are better with every passing year.

• POTATOES AND SWEET POTATOES

Potatoes and sweet potatoes are perhaps the most commonly barbecued vegetables, particularly when cooked unpeeled, directly atop the embers or "leaded" (wrapped in aluminum foil). Give them a try in either style, served with a bit of butter and salt, or with a generous tablespoon of "criolla" sauce.

• CORN

To barbecue corn there are at least two options. The first is to peel them, add butter and salt, wrap them in aluminum foil and place them on the grill at a medium heat, until the corn is tender. The second option is to remove the beard, pull down the husk (without removing the leaves), spread butter and salt and re-wrap them with their leaves and grill them on a low fire for about half an hour. An ideal option to entertain hungry guests until the meat is ready.

• EGGPLANTS

Before taking the eggplants to the grill, you need to wash them and cut them in halves (not slices, and lengthwise, not across). Make superficial crisscross cuts and place them on the hot grill with the skin side down. Once grilled, you can complement their delicious flavor with a bit of olive oil or a sauce of your concoction (note: they do taste wonderful with mayonnaise mixed with minced garlic, parsley, salt and pepper). You can also cut the eggplants in long slices about one centimeter thick and cook them over the grill until golden, sprinkling them with just a bit of olive oil and salt.

• PEPPERS AND SQUASH

For peppers and squash (as with carrots, onions, potatoes and sweet potatoes), the procedure is easy: prepare a fire with hardwood logs and once you've got good embers place the vegetables, still with their skins on (or well wrapped on aluminum foil) directly in the fire and cover them with embers. Keep in mind you have to have plenty of embers so the meat on top of the grill won't lose any heat. After a bit more than half an hour, they will be ready to be removed, skinned, sliced in half, seasoned with your choice of condiments (olive oil, salt, butter) and turned into a fine memory. If you prefer, you can also cook peppers, squash and onions sliced in half atop the grill. It's really up to you.

Chimichurri:
the Argentine sauce

Many different sauces can be christened with the name of "chimichurri" though, truth be told, they are, strictly speaking, "adobos." And to the many basic variations, add those created with total impunity by barbecue cooks all over the country, when they follow their whims by adding, eliminating, or reducing the amount of ingredients. To be true to form and make good "chimichurri" you need only mix your ingredients in a bottle or jar and leave the container alone in a cool place for two to four days, until all the flavors are properly blended, before using it. Some folks, preferring a milder sauce, make the "chimichurri" just before using it. Many would consider it a sin to add "chimichurri" to the meat, meat with its hide, lamb, or goat while grilling. Really, though, it's up to you. The most advisable thing, is probably to place it in a sauce pan so each guest can make up his or her mind.

INGREDIENTS: **SALMUERA** (salt dissolved in water), **HALF A CUP** | **OIL, 4 TABLESPOONS** | **WINE VINEGAR, 1 CUP** | **GARLIC, 5 CLOVES** ground in a mortar | **LAUREL, 4 LEAVES** | **OREGANO: TO TASTE** | **BLACK PEPPER, 1 TEASPOON** | **MINCED PEPPERS, 4 TABLESPOONS**

"Criolla" sauce, typical and tasty

"Criolla" sauce recipes there are many; with the best having the following ingredients. Dice everything very small and mix with oil, vinegar, salt and pepper.

INGREDIENTS: RED PEPPER, 1 | GREEN PEPPER, 1 | ONION, 1 | TOMATOES: 2 | OIL: 1 CUP | VINEGAR, HALF A CUP | PARSLEY LEAVES, HALF A CUP | SALT | PEPPER

Green Sauce
and Walnut Sauce

Although no longer among the most traditional condiments, the green sauce deserves to recover a privileged position next to our wooden plates and "asados de tira" (short ribs, bone in). Its preparation couldn't be easier: mix all ingredients in a blender or mixer and let technology take over until the mixture acquires the consistency of a sauce. Keep in mind that green sauce is ideal not only to accompany a barbecue but also for "puchero" (meat stew).

INGREDIENTS: **PARSLEY, OR PARSLEY AND BASIL, A BIG BUNCH** | **WHITE BREAD,** without crust, **2 SLICES** | **COOKED EGG YOLKS, 2** | **GARLIC CLOVES, 2** | **SALT AND PEPPER, TO TASTE** | **OLIVE OIL, 1 CUP** | **VINEGAR, HALF A CUP**

Walnut sauce will bring a smile to those who've tired of more conventional dressings. Place the walnuts in a deep pot and cover them with previously boiled milk – already cold. In a different pot, wet the bread (without crust) with some more milk. Dice the garlic cloves and mash the walnuts until they turn into a smooth paste. Mix the paste with the bread and the garlic. Add salt and pepper to taste, add a touch of olive oil, another of hot water and mix well until all ingredients are blended. The walnut sauce, or nougat sauce not only goes well with the barbecue, it also provides an excellent excuse, the following day, to taste some of the leftover cold red meat.

INGREDIENTS: **PEELED WALNUTS, 300 GRAMS** | **FRENCH BREAD, 1/2 KG** | **MILK, AS NEEDED** | **GARLIC CLOVES, 2** | **OIL, TWO TABLESPOONS** | **SALT AND PEPPER, TO TASTE**

Barbecued Cheese

For many, barbecued cheese is a luxury that cannot be absent from the barbecue preliminaries. "Provoleta" is a local version, with flavor similar to the Italian Provolone.

So that the provoleta won't melt and disappear between the grill's rails, you'll need to let the slices sit at room temperature for at least an hour. If you didn't buy provoletas already seasoned, you can choose from among different ingredients to round up its flavor: olive oil, oregano, ground pepper, or a combination of the three. To cook it, the grill must be very hot. You can decide whether you want to flip it directly over the grill (highly recommended) or let it melt and cook to a crisp inside an aluminum pan.

Empanadas (meat pies) from Salta Province

T here is a recipe for "empanadas" (meat pies) for every region or province in Argentina. But this delicacy's stronghold is the Northwest, where they're made both juicy and spicy. Nearly eighty per cent of the recipes call for meat, but rest assured: what follows is not just one recipe among many. It's an infallible combination.

Meat for the stuffing should be cut with a knife into small pieces. That is the chief trick for juicy empanadas: ground meat dries up much faster. After cutting, you need to heat up the fat (or oil), sauté the onions and add the meat. As soon as it browns, remove it from the heat. Add the potatoes, the hardboiled eggs, the olives, the raisins and the condiments. There are those who

prefer the shortcut of packaged shells, useful for an emergency, but a certain failure if you want to leave a mark on the memory of your guests. To do that, you'll need to start the shells from scratch. Work the dough made with lard, flour and "salmuera" (salted water) until it's soft, and then let it rest, covered with a clean piece of cloth. The rest is the familiar story: stretch the dough, cut it in circles and distribute the stuffing, do the folding, paint them with beaten egg and cook them in a hot oven until golden. According to etiquette, they must be eaten without utensils, protecting the hand from the hot meat with a napkin. Before the first bite, experts suggest shaking the empanada to distribute the juices inside.

CLASSIC MEAT STUFFING:**MEAT, HALF A KG**
Use "carnaza" (silverside), roast-beef, "bola de lomo" (sirloin tip), "tortuguita" (leg beef) or "lomo" (tenderloin) **|REFINED BEEF LARD OR PORK LARD, 200 GRAMS |GREEN ONIONS, HALF A KG |GROUND SWEET PEPPER, ONE AND A HALF TABLESPOON |POTATOES,** big, cooked and diced, **2 |RAISINS, 100 GRAMS |OLIVES,** diced, **ONE AND A HALF DOZEN |EGGS,** hardboiled, **DICED, 3 |SALT, GROUND PEPPER, PEPPER, TO TASTE**

DOUGH (FOR BAKING):**FLOUR, 750 GRAMS |LARD, WARM, 150 GRAMS** (if you can get it, "pella" lard is recommended)

"Picadita" (hors d'oeuvres) and Empanadas (meat pies)

Because the barbecue takes time and knowing how to wait for it is part of being successful, you'll need strategies to distract anxious and hungry guests, so you won't undergo the pressure of their insistent staring at the sweaty meat on the grill.

The "picada" (hors d'oeuvres), a classic strategy among classics, allows as ingredients, practically anything that crosses your mind or that was left orphaned in the refrigerator.

In theory, it just depends on your ability to disguise leftovers and enhance canned food. Traditionalists will, of course, pontificate that practically the only thing allowed in a gauchos' gathering would be "salame de campo" (homemade salami), a table of cheeses, and homemade bread. But others will consider olives, potato chips, peanuts, pâté and pickled meat and vegetables. Your call.

Empanadas, on the other side, are an undisputed prologue to "criollo" barbecues. Of course you can offer empanadas you've bought, but if laziness doesn't get the best of you and you want to put your best foot forward, you will find what follows a perfect recipe for traditional "empanadas" (meat pies).

The important thing when it comes to preliminaries: be exact in your calculations and proportions, so as not to ruin your guests' appetites. That way, the barbecue, the feast's true attraction, won't loose its starring role.

Salads

With salads, everything depends on the preference and imagination of whoever is preparing them. Among the types of salad that cannot be absent are, of course, a lettuce, tomato and onion salad, a potato and hard-boiled eggs salad, and a potato and parsley salad. Nonetheless, your vegetable table may offer such equally interesting options as the potato and onions with mayonnaise salad; peppers, tomatoes and onions salad; or other combinations, like diced peppers and rice; or rice, peas and parsley. If you or your guests are willing to try novelty combinations, you may go for a spinach, champignon mushrooms and bacon bits salad; or a rugula, blue cheese and pears salad; or a deliciously refreshing leeks and honeydew melon salad.

The star of this section will be, just for today, the golden onion salad. To prepare it you will need: four big onions, two tablespoons of olive oil, two teaspoonfuls of sugar, three tablespoons of vinegar, salt and pepper to taste and a tablespoon of soy sauce.

Peel the onions and cut them in fourths. Cook them in a pan with the olive oil for ten to fifteen minutes on a medium stove (cover the pan, and stir occasionally). After this initial period, sprinkle the onions with sugar and continue cooking (always with the pan covered) for ten more minutes, stirring continuously. Then add the vinegar, salt and pepper and cook for yet another ten to fifteen minutes. Uncover the pan; add three tablespoons of water (to loosen the juices that have adhered to the pan) and the soy sauce. Remove from the fire and let cool in a serving bowl. A quick and truly delicious dish to interrupt the routine of vegetable tables.

Wine

South Americans, the upper classes in particular, are very sober, and if they occasionally commit excesses in their dining, succumbing to the irresistible temptation of a good barbecue, a stew, or a delicious fricassee, it is enough for them to drink just two or three glasses of wine.

J. P. & W. P. ROBERTSON, LETTERS FROM SOUTH AMERICA

I n every kingdom there are princes. And if in the world of barbecues, meat rules, wine, no doubt, is the leader of the princes. There are many options, and what you choose depends on the creativity, the willingness to experiment, or the more traditional or orthodox tendencies of your palate.

In principle, it's worth mentioning that the best wine to accompany a barbecue of red meats is a red wine. Within the reds, the best are those well aged and strong of body, say, a Malbec. Nothing should prevent you, however, from leaning towards a Cabernet Sauvignon of good color and better aroma. And a Syrah, with a well defined and refreshing acidity would be ideal to accompany lamb, while a fruity Malbec would be the perfect companion for the "picada" – hors d'oeuvres. Your barbecue may include fish, and in that case, white wines should be taken into consideration.

Of course, with the intricate combination of entrails, red meats, white meats, sausages, cheeses and vegetables that make up a true barbecue, options and debate can last until the wee hours of the morning. If your friends and family are demanding, and you want to make everybody happy, the best thing would be to organize a "tasting" barbecue and offer different types of wine (no more than four options, unless you expect your guests to request extra mattresses to spend the night) and wait for the verdicts during the conversation.

Wine not only accompanies the guests, it is also the cook's basic ally. If your guests know what's good for them, your glass will always be full and your criterion will be the defining one when it's time to choose a specific winery or vintage.

Mate

The gaucho's first distraction, once he's done with his exhausting labor is mate. For that reason, as soon as they were done with their duties, men could be seen filling their mates or sucking through the metal straws "bombillas", while they slowly walk around.

J. P. & W. P. ROBERTSON, LETTERS FROM SOUTH AMERICA

If we didn't have a flag, or passports, or lapel pins, and the Argentinian spread out all over the world had to recognize each other without the benefit of words; if it were necessary to find a fondness on which the thirty plus million who inhabit this land can agree; if we needed an indisputable element to define our idiosyncrasy; if the gastronomic history of our country demanded a single representative… well, mate and barbecue would have to argue for a long time before either could take the top position on the podium.

Nevertheless, when it's time to light the fire, spend a day in the country or with a gathering of friends and family, both elements manage to coexist convivially and generously accompany each other. During the long waiting hours, while getting the fire ready before staking the goat or lamb on the grill, during the endless afternoons after the siesta and the digestive processes that turn the barbecue into a pleasant memory, mate makes its entrance and fills any potentially uncomfortable silence. So how could we not give it, in this book, the place it rightfully deserves?

As with any ceremony full of the symbolic values, for an idiosyncrasy as complex as that of Argentinian, mate has also its secrets and you must know them to please the most demanding and critical of your guests.

Mate: Bitter or "cimarrón"

S ome people let the water boil so the mate won't get cold after the first round, while others maintain that with boiled water, the yerba mate gets burned. You may prefer the metal straw – the "bombilla" – to be curved and the water warm; your neighbor may swear that the yerba mate without stems and very hot water is preferable. Some folks add orange peels or coffee grounds, others make it with milk or flavored yerba mate. The options are endless and when it comes to taste there's nothing written in stone.

For this reason it is impossible to give much advice without generating disagreement. We'll merely describe the steps for pouring a bitter mate for the connoisseur – one that doesn't get "washed out" and can be enjoyed by each of the participants in the drinking circle. First, fill the gourd with yerba mate to only two-thirds of its capacity. Cover the opening with your hand and flip it over (this way you'll separate the yerba mate on one side, while the dust – which some people say is not healthy – will collect on the palm of your hand). Moisten the mate on the side of the mate gourd that has less yerba mate with warm water (so the yerba mate will swell up and won't get burned when you pour hot water). After it's well soaked, you can introduce the "bombilla" and pour the water hot but never boiled (approximately 80° C) into the gourd. It is important to pour the water in thin streams, against the "bombilla" from six or seven centimeters high, so it will reach all the yerba mate without "washing it out." When the yerba mate gets washed out – you'll see the little stems floating on the surface – you must then change it, either in its entirety or just a portion of the yerba already used, replacing it with fresh one.

Keep in mind that a well-poured mate will always be foamy.

And don't forget, for barbecues, as in a good mate circle, everybody will be happy if they feel their every whim has been attended to. Everything depends, thus, on your knowledge and experience, but also on your abilities as a host.